SIBLING REVELRY!

Celebrating the fun of being a brother or a sister

BY GRACE WITWER HOUSHOLDER
ILLUSTRATED BY DEBBIE RITTENHOUSE

Humor
Inspirational
Parenting

QUOTABLE KIDS: FUN IN THE FAMILY TREE
(Sibling Revelry & Parent "Releaf")

Published by The Funny Kids Project, 816 Mott Street, Kendallville, IN 46755 USA
www.funnykids.com

Text © 2000 by Grace Witwer Housholder
Illustrations © 2000 by Debbie Rittenhouse
Cover, text design © 2000 Tamara Dever, TLC Graphics and Erin Stark, Stark Design Works

Quote by Mary Schmich courtesy of the Chicago Tribune

Publisher's Cataloging-in-Publication
  (Provided by Quality Books, Inc.)

Housholder, Grace Witwer.
      Quotable kids : fun in the family tree / Grace
  Witwer Housholder ; illustrated by Debbie
  Rittenhouse. -- 1st ed.
      p. cm.
      CONTENTS: Sibling revelry -- Parent releaf.
      ISBN: 0-9663006-1-0

      1. Family--Quotations. 2. Family--Humor. 3.
  Children--Quotations. 4. Children--Humor. 5.
  Upside-down books--Specimens.   I. Rittenhouse,
  Debbie.   II. Title.

PN6231.F3H58 2000   306.85'0207
                    QBI00-217

Printed byBang Printing, Brainerd, MN, USA

ACKNOWLEDGEMENTS

Many people deserve a big thank you for their part
in helping this book to become a reality.

Thank you to Debbie Rittenhouse for
her wonderful illustrations;

to Tami Dever and Erin Stark for taking our ideas
and creating something we can all be proud of;

to Hilda Studebaker for suggesting this format;

to my daughter Liz for her insightful comments;

to my husband Terry for his ongoing support;

and to the thousands of people around the world
who have contributed and continue to contribute
stories to The Funny Kids Project.

*Proceeds from the sale of our books are donated
to charities that help children and families.*

This book
belongs to

For Sally, Vi and George

• •

"Be like one
big happy family ...
loving one another
with tender hearts ... "

INTRODUCTION

Revelry means celebration and merry-making.
But anyone who has one or more brothers or sisters
knows that being a sibling is not always a party …
it can range from slugfest to spying to sharing secrets
or stealing underwear. Sibling Revelry means:

R – Ready for your sibling?

E – Evaluating your sibling

V – Vanquishing your sibling

E – Educating your sibling

L – Learning with your sibling

R – Roughhousing with your sibling

Y – Yet we are family forever!

"Sibling Revelry" is about the excitement, anticipation and apprehension prior to the arrival of a new brother or sister, the mixed emotions that come after the sibling is born, the inevitable squabbles and fights, the exchanges of ideas and advice … but, above all, the humor that pops up at the most unexpected times. I hope this book helps you to savor and save the fun times … and to laugh — or at least smile — at the times that weren't so great. Remember to fill in the pages in the middle of this book with some of your favorite memories of "sibling revelry" to create a volume that will grow in sentimental value over the years!

Grace Witwer Housholder
Funny Kids Project
Kendallville, Indiana, USA
www.funnykids.com

• •

"Be nice to your siblings.
They're your best link to your past
and the people most likely to stick with you
in the future."

MARY SCHMICH

• •

READY FOR YOUR SIBLING?

Emotions about the pending arrival of a new sibling range from offering playthings for the unborn brother or sister to packing up and preparing for a quick get-away ...

When his mother was pregnant, Adam, 3, asked what the baby did in there. Cynthia told him the baby ate, slept and sucked his thumb. Adam brought her a handful of Matchbox cars. "Eat them for dinner," he told his mother, "so the baby has something to play with!"

MARK ASKED HIS MOTHER when his new little brother would be arriving. "Soon," she replied. Mark went to his bedroom and returned with his backpack. "I'm running away," Mark announced. His mother held out her arms and said, "Give me a hug first." Then she continued, "Now Mark, I am sorry you are running away. It's not safe out there." Mark gave his mother a big hug and said, "Don't worry, Mom. I'll stay on the sidewalk!"

RITA WAS TELLING SAMMY, 3, that she was going to have a baby. Sammy asked, "Who is going to be the mommy and daddy of the baby?" Rita said, "Well, we are of course!" Sammy was indignant: "But you are my mommy, and Daddy is my daddy!"

Amanda, 4: Daddy got you pregnant, didn't he?

Wanda: Yes!

Amanda: How did he do it?

Wanda: You'll learn that when you get older.

Amanda: Was it magic?

Wanda: It was kinda like magic.

Amanda: So he just said, "I want Mommy to be pregnant" and you got pregnant?

Wanda (laughing): Something like that.

Amanda (worried): Uh-oh, Mommy. You might have two babies, because I said the same thing!

A LITTLE BOY TOLD HIS MOTHER that the minute he gets married he's going to the hospital. "The hospital?" the mother asked. "Yes, to pick out a baby!"

WHEN JACOB TOLD HIS THIRD-GRADE CLASS that his mother was expecting, Amanda asked him what he wanted the baby to be. "A boy," Jacob said. "What does your sister want?" Amanda asked. "A girl," Jacob said. "What does your mom want the baby to be?" "The last one," Jacob said.

A FATHER OF THREE explained the facts of life to his 9-year-old son, with not a little embarrassment. When the father was done, the boy looked at him with amazement. "You and mom did that THREE times?" he said.

A PREGNANT MOTHER was telling her 5-year-old about the baby that was growing inside her. She pointed to various parts of her abdomen and said, "Here's the head. Here's the feet. ..."

Later the 5-year-old asked, "If the head is over here and the feet over there, who's going to put it together?"

TYLER, 7, made some new friends who were twins. One day he asked his mother, "How do you get twins?" She told him that the egg divides and there are two babies. "Gee," Tyler said, "I wish my egg would have broken."

CINDY TRIED TO PREPARE Hilary, 3, for the arrival of her new brother. One day Hilary was playing with her favorite blanket. Suddenly she looked at her mother and said, "I'm going to share my baby brother with my blanket!"

WHEN DIANE FOUND out she was pregnant, she told the good news to anyone who would listen. But her 4-year-old overheard some of her parents' private conversations. One day when Diane and her 4-year-old were shopping, a woman asked the little girl if she was excited about the new baby. "Oh, yes!" the 4-year-old said, "and I know what we are going to name it. If it's a girl we're going to call her Christina, and if it's a boy we're going to call it quits!"

· 7 ·

WHEN CODY WAS 4, he was told that there was a baby in Mommy's tummy. He also knew that at one time he had been in Mommy's tummy, too. It never crossed his parents' minds that Cody had to figure out how he and his little brother Caleb could both be in Mommy's tummy. When he was 6, Cody asked his father if he remembered "when you met Mommy and wanted to kiss her and get married and I was in her tummy and Caleb was in her leg!"

KLANCI'S MOTHER WAS expecting. When Klanci's preschool teacher heard the news, she said, "Are you going to get a new brother or sister in your family?"

"No, I think I'll keep my old ones," Klanci said.

EVALUATING YOUR SIBLING

When the new baby arrives, there are a lot of adjustments to be made by everyone — especially siblings. And it doesn't help that the baby isn't ready yet to play ball. As the months and years go by, siblings are constantly comparing and/or evaluating each other and competing for Mom and Dad's time, attention and maybe even inheritance. It's at those times that parents pray for the patience of Job and the wisdom of Solomon!

Phillip, who said he didn't want a sister, was excited to learn that his mom had given birth to a brother. When he got to see his new baby brother, he looked right at his mom and said with great disappointment, "That's a baby — not a brother!"

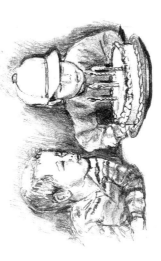

OUT OF THE BLUE IAN, 7, asked his mom, "When you and Dad die, who gets all your stuff?" Startled by the question, Ann decided to answer the question with a question. "Why?" Ann asked. "Is there something you want?" "Yes," Ian said, "I want Dad's pocket knife." "Well, Evan, is there something your want?" Ann asked her younger son. "Yes," Evan said quickly, "I'll take the money!"

WHEN HOLLY BEGAN WALKING, she would sneak up behind Ryan, grab one of his toys and then take off running. One day Ryan had had enough of it and told Linda, "You need to take her back, and get one that doesn't walk!"

A MOTHER WAS NURSING her newborn when her son burst into the room. He opened his eyes wide. The mother had no choice but to explain to him how God had given her milk to feed the baby. She added that later she would give the baby orange juice, also. "Is that what's in the other one?" the little boy asked.

A MOTHER RECEIVED a phone call while she was nursing. Her 7-year-old told the caller, "She can't come to the phone now. She's milking the baby."

DANIEL, 3, and Colton, 4, were carrying on a conversation while using the urinals in a public restroom.
"Mine is the Tasmanian Devil!" one boy said.
"Mine is Superman!" the other boy said.
They were comparing the prints on their underwear!

EMILY, 4, and Lillian, 3, had this conversation:

Emily: Lillian, what do you want to be when you grow up?

Lillian: Six.

BEFORE SUE WENT to Hawaii she asked her granddaughter, Olivia, 5, what she wanted Grandma to bring back for her.

"A two-halfer bathing suit!" Olivia said.

"Does your brother want a bathing suit, too?" Sue asked.

"No, he only wears a one-halfer!" Olivia said.

EMILY, 2, had just soiled her diaper.

"Go to Mommy and get your diaper changed," Ben, 4, said.

"It is not dirty," Emily said.

"Is too," Ben said.

"Is not!"

Totally exasperated, Ben said, "Look at me! Why am I arguing with someone half my age?"

JEFF, 3, told his older brother Chuck that he was never going to sin again. Chuck told him that it's not possible to stop sinning because everybody sins. "But my sins will be good sins," Jeff said.

EIGHT-MONTH-OLD ARYN was sitting on the floor screaming. His dad said jokingly, "Is all that noise necessary?" Aryn's 2-year-old brother looked very seriously at his dad and said, "No, that's Aryn."

ONE NIGHT AS THE children crowded around the table to eat, Ethan, 2, didn't dig in as usual. Gerry saw that he was looking down and around the table. Finally Ethan looked up and said, "Why am I the only one who has plastic under their chair?"

TOM, KATIE'S OLDER BROTHER, was listening as Katie spelled words out loud. The first word was "Christmas." The second word was "like." Then she started spelling another longer word.

"That's not a word," Tom said.

Katie insisted that it was.

Katie's mother asked her to repeat what she had spelled.

Katie said "c-a-l-f-l-i-c-k."

"The first part is a word and the second part is a word," Katie's mother said, "but together the two words don't say anything."

"Yes sir, Mom," Katie said, "It is what we are — calflicks!"

VANQUISHING YOUR SIBLING

Siblings may be best friends. But there comes a time in every kid's life — sometimes several times a day — that you have to assert your dominance over your siblings.

Arguing over silly and/or earthshaking things or wishing your sibling would vanish are a normal part of growing up.

"Let the
little children
come to me."

WHEN CHRISTOPHER started going to preschool, he discovered that his younger brother Jacob knew exactly what to say to annoy him. After preschool Christopher, sounding very superior, asked Jacob what he did all day while he was at school. Jacob put on a Mona Lisa smile, swaggered a bit, and said calmly, "I play with YOUR TOYS!"

SCOTT, 6, wanted his mother to help him with something, but Cathie said she was busy with Sam, 2. After Cathie repeatedly told Scott she was busy with Sam, Scott commanded: "Sell him!"

EVERY DAY WHEN PAM picked up her daughters, Heather and Hilary, the two girls started bickering.

"Every afternoon when I pick you up, I pray that you won't argue in the car," Pam wearily told the girls one day.

"Well, keep on praying," Heather said.

KRISTEN, 9, and Staci, 8, were having an argument in the back seat of the car. Janet was carefully watching them in the rearview mirror. She saw Staci pinch Kristen. Kristen then hit Staci, causing her to yell, "Mom … Kristen hit me!"

"But you started it," Janet said.

"I did not."

"I don't think you're telling the truth."

"Fine," Staci replied, "when you die, ask God!"

STEVEN AND CHAD were playing ball. When their mother asked them who won, Steven said, "Well, the score was 7 to more. Chad got 7 and I got more!"

ALEXANDER, 3, came to his uncle with messy pants. Richard scolded him, but Alexander would not admit guilt. "Ava did it," Alexander said with a straight face. Ava was his sister.

AT MIDNIGHT when Marcia came home from work, she noticed a trail of popcorn leading from the kitchen up the stairs to her 7-year-old daughter's room. The next morning Marcia asked why there was a trail of popcorn. Her 4-year-old giggled and responded, "so if a monster comes into our house at night, he would eat the popcorn and be in Laura's room and eat her instead of me!"

AT THE PRE-SEASON Little League tourney a very young, new batter stepped to the plate. He clutched his bat and looked terrified. A 12-year-old girl, who obviously was his adoring older sister, yelled to him, "Swing, you can do it!" The boy clutched his bat and didn't swing. The sister yelled again, "You can do it, SWING!" The ball went by again. Strike two. As the pitcher wound up a third time, the sister yelled in desperation, "Think of it as if it were me. SWING!"

WHILE LEE WAS PREPARING the Thanksgiving turkey, Grace, 2, started patting the bird, saying, "Tur-kee, tur-kee." Grace must have seen a resemblance between the 15-pound bird and her new baby sister, because while continuing to pat the turkey, she started saying, "Bay-bee, bay-bee." When Lee put the turkey in the oven, Grace said, with a sly smile on her face, "Night night, bay-bee!"

SIX SIBLINGS AND THEIR PARENTS were seated

around the dinner table. Eyes closed. Hands held.
With the exception of father, they were anxiously awaiting
the completion of the prayer. Mother's mashed potatoes and
gravy had a way of distracting them from whatever father
happened to mention in his prayers. Immediately upon
hearing the long-awaited "amen," Jimmy, 3, belted out,
"Dad ... Dad! Brenda had her eyes open during your prayer."
The 4-year-old's face dropped and her shoulders caved in as
she awaited her reprimand.

But, instead, father asked, "Jimmy, how is it that you know
that your sister had her eyes open during the prayer?"

Shocked by the frightening question, Jimmy thought for a
second or two, then blurted out, "I heard them open!"

BROOKE, 5, had been fighting with Lacey. Brooke told her mother Lacey needs glasses.

"Why?" her mother asked in surprise.

"Because she saw me doing things I wasn't doing!"

ABBEY WAS TRYING to spin a half-dollar. Erin picked it up and commented that there was a guy's picture on one side and an eagle on the other. Abbey grabbed it back and snarled, "No, it's not. It's heads on one side and toes on the other!"

KATHIE WAS HAVING a serious talk with Jimmy, 6, who had perfected the art of teasing his younger brother, Mark, to the point of tears. "Jimmy," she said, "I want you to really think about how much you tease Mark. It's becoming a habit." "It's not a habit," Jimmy retorted. "It's a hobby!"

SARAH, 5, and Kathryn, 2, were playing with their Barbie dolls. Sarah had her Barbie family in a marked-off area called her "neighborhood." When Kathryn walked through her neighborhood to get a toy, Sarah became very upset. "Kathryn, you're always bugging me," she said. "Don't ever step in my neighborhood again!" Kathryn's face puckered up, and she left the room.

Grandma Violet, whose husband is a pastor, admonished Sarah. "Honey," Violet said, "I don't think Kathryn is trying to bug you. She looks up to you, and she wants to be like you. If you want her to be nice to you, you can show her by being a good example." "What book did you get that out of?" Sarah asked.

DeANNA, 3, was acting up at the dinner table. Wanting to give her a warning about her attitude, her father said, "DeAnna, who wants a spanking?" Without batting an eyelash, DeAnna looked at her older sister, Debi, and said, "Debi."

EDUCATING YOUR SIBLING

Who's your most persistent,
particular and pompous professor?
Probably your sibling!

Joe, 1, was standing
in his high chair.
"Sit down, Joe,"
his 2-year-old
sister said. "You
might fall down and
bump your head and have to go to
the doctor and he might find one of your
batteries missing."

FRED WAS SITTING in church with Scott, 6, and Dustin, 10. They had taken communion and were waiting for the rest of the congregation to finish. Scott moved over closer to Fred. Dustin, thinking Scott was trying to get out of the pew, said, "No, Scott, you don't get to go back for seconds!"

RANDY AND SANDRA were trying to teach their 7-year-old son "The Lord's Prayer" when little brother Jared spoke up, "I've got it ... My father does art work in heaven!"

DEBBI WAS NURSING BABY FAITH when Anna, 5, came into the room. When Faith turned to look at her sister, her ear was by Debbi's breast. "Silly Faith," Anna said. "Mommy can't feed you through your ear. The milk will come out the other side!"

AXEL, 8, took some swimming lessons that included simple CPR training. He learned that if a person is choking, you should say, "Keep coughing!"

The next day at lunch Axel's older brother started coughing. Axel jumped up and yelled, "Keep choking! Keep choking!"

LOGAN, 5, said that when he goes to bed he lies awake all night and never sleeps. Jayden asked, "Well, what do you do all night?" Logan replied, "I just lie there and watch my dreams!"

KATIE AND HER LITTLE BROTHER Ben were talking about what heaven will be like. Ben said the lights in heaven will be on all the time. "There aren't any lights in heaven," Katie said. "Yes, there are!" The siblings argued back and forth, until Ben said triumphantly, "Yes, there are — the Israelites!"

WENDY WAS TRYING to get Jacob to sign up for a summer ball team. She was telling him how much fun he would have. Little Rebecca overheard the conversation and said, "Jacob, what Mom is saying is that you need plenty of fresh air and sunshine."

"I WANT TO GO TO COLLEGE because it makes you smarter and you can get a better job," Kerstinn, 6, told her grandparents. Kollienn, 4, said she wanted to go to college, too. "But not to get smarter," she said. "I'm going to college to turn cartwheels!"

TWO SISTERS GOT INTO their mother's van after being very physically active. Each girl accused the other of smelling sweaty. The younger one started crying. "It's OK," the older one said, trying to comfort her. "Your horizontals (hormones) go crazy at your age, but in a few years they'll be OK!"

KRISTY, 13, was having a conversation with her little sister Cassie, 3. "Where do you live?" Kristy asked. With a look that showed she wondered why Kristy would ask such a simple question, Cassie said, "Duh, at Mommy's house!" Kristy asked Cassie if it was Daddy's house, too. "No, Daddy's house is right there," Cassie said. And she pointed to the family's new garage!

CHUCK, 9, and Jeff, 8, were discussing whether people live in Antarctica. "But there's nothing there," Chuck reasoned. "How would they get stuff to live?" After a thoughtful pause, Jeff said, "UPS!"

LUCY, 7, and Dorothy Lee, 5, were playing with Chuck while he was seated in his high chair. They had placed a doll in the high chair with Chuck and utensils so that Chuck could feed the doll. "We're teaching Chuck to be a daddy," they told their mother in unison.

PAUL, 6, was in a pet store with his big sister. Paul struck up a conversation with a parrot … a series of hellos from the parrot to Paul and from Paul to the parrot. Paul asked his sister if she would buy the robot bird. "That's not a robot bird," she said. "It's a real bird." "No, it's a robot," Paul said. "Birds can't talk."

CASSIE, 3, was playing in her sandbox. She got carried away, and all the sand ended up on a mat by the back door. Her brother told her to brush the mat. "I can't," Cassie said. "I don't have any toothpaste!"

A 7-YEAR-OLD and a 10-year-old were watching their mother put on eye liner while she was preparing for a formal affair. "Why are you putting that on?" the 7-year-old asked. "So she can look older," the 10-year-old said in a know-it-all tone of voice.

WHILE THEIR MOTHER was putting a lattice crust on a pie, Melissa, 3, asked, "Mommy, why are you putting seatbelts on the pie?" Her older sister responded, "So that while it's cooking the apples won't fall out when it bubbles!"

DEREK, 5, came home from kindergarten with a tooth in an envelope. Annette hugged him and told him they would put the tooth under his pillow that night for the Tooth Fairy. "You really expect me to believe that some funny looking person dressed in a pink tutu comes into my room at night and takes my old tooth and leaves me a dollar?" Derek asked. "I'm in kindergarten now, Mom! I don't believe in baby stories anymore." "Oh no!" Annette said. "If you don't believe in the Tooth Fairy I guess we'll just throw it away and you won't get anything but a new tooth in its place. I'm so sorry, I thought you were a believer." Annette walked out of the room and took the envelope with her. A few minutes later she heard Derek talking to Lisa, 9. "Derek, you dummy!" Lisa said. "Do you know how many dollars I got from the Tooth Fairy? I got enough to buy a Barbie. Think of all the money you won't get. Think of that new 'Star Wars' toy you want."
A minute late Derek came back to Annette and said, "Hey Mom, about that Tooth Fairy thing. I forgot, I thought you meant that other fairy, you know like on 'Oz.' I believe in the Tooth Fairy. I hope you still have my old tooth!"

WHILE DRIVING, LaRea noticed a groundhog and pointed it out to her little sister, Niccole. A little while later LaRea pointed out a woodchuck to Niccole. Niccole started eagerly looking for nature on her own. After a few minutes she called out, "Oh, there's a ground chuck!"

AN 11-YEAR-OLD RECEIVED some popcorn that was still on the ear of the corn. She put the ear of corn in the microwave to pop the kernels. Then she called to her younger brother, "Come and get some popcorn made just like the Indians used to make it!"

DOROTHY, 11, decided to teach her little brother, Paul, 3, how to play Ping-Pong. She instructed Liz, 9, and Catherine, 5, to cheer for their little brother no matter what he did so that he would feel good about himself. Dorothy served to Paul. He swung with all his might and missed. "Hurray!" Liz and Catherine cheered. "That not 'hurray!'" Paul said indignantly. "That strike one!"

THE KIDS STARTED talking about ballet and how the dancers wear leotards. The question came up, "What do you call men who dance in a ballet? You don't call them ballerinas, so what do you call them?" Zachary-Taylor, 9, said, "They call 'em Robin Hoods!"

LEARNING WITH YOUR SIBLING

Long-lasting lessons are learned with love and laughter!

Alex, 7, went to his sister's bedroom one night and asked, "Is God our father?" Ashley, 14, replied, "Yes, God is our father." Alex thought for a minute, turned toward the door and said, "Hmmm ... I wonder if Mom knows about this!"

DAWNE WAS PREPARING to give a talk on unity at her women's Bible study. She woke up early to type out the scripture verses. She wasn't quite finished when her four children began coming downstairs asking for breakfast. She could hear the children just around the corner in the kitchen as they rummaged through the refrigerator and cupboards for something to eat. At some point they discovered half of a toaster pastry on the counter from the night before. They all began screaming and fighting; each claiming the half-eaten Pop Tart. As Dawne made a couple of futile attempts to quiet them, she finished typing the verse in Matthew 5:9 that says, "Blessed are the peacemakers for they shall be called sons of God." Taking her cue from scripture, she hollered into the kitchen above the din, "Would somebody PLEASE be the peacemaker?!" There was a moment's silence and then Garret, 6, piped up, "I'll be the piece maker, Mom!" Then to his brother and sisters he said: "Here's a piece for you and you, and a piece for you and one piece for me." Dawne had her opening illustration on unity and peace for that evening's Bible study!

JARROD, Evy, Seagan and Nick went trick or treating at Dr. Warrener's house. As the doctor's son passed out the treats, the children's father told them that the boy handing out treats was the son of the man who brought all four of them into the world. "What!" Jarrod, 5, exclaimed. "He's JESUS!"

PHILLIP, 9, was reading the ingredients label on his older sister's make-up. "Not tested on animals," Phillip read. "Duhhhhh. When do dogs wear blush?"

WHEN HIS LITTLE BROTHER was battling chicken pox, Evan, 5, reported to friends: "Trey is turning into a Dalmatian!"

SCOTT, 4, and Kevin, 2, like to listen to tapes while their mother is driving them in the van. One day Scott asked his mother to put on the "diaper song." Kathy has lots of kids' songs in the van, but that request didn't sound familiar so she asked Scott to sing the song. Scott sang, "Jesus diapered all the children …" After she had recovered, Kathy explained the song is, "Jesus died for all the children." But Scott still sings, "Jesus diapered all the children." He told his mother it's happier!

BEN, 5, and Josh, 4, went to church with their aunt. The boys' church doesn't have a choir, just congregational singing. When the choir entered in their white robes, Josh leaned over and said to Ben, "Are those angels?" Ben, the all-knowing big brother, replied, "Naw, they don't have those circles around their heads."

LAURA AND PATTY shared a bedroom. When Laura lost a tooth, she placed it under her pillow. The next morning her tooth was gone and some money was in its place. Patty went quietly up to her mother and said, "Mommy, I know who the Tooth Fairy is … I saw you put money under Laura's pillow last night when she was asleep." Rather surprised, her mother replied, "Well, I guess you're right. I was the Tooth Fairy." Patty thought for a moment and with a big grin on her face said, "Now if you're the Tooth Fairy, then Daddy must be God!"

MAX, 7, had shrimp cocktail with his older brother and loved it. But apparently he didn't know the name of what he was eating. When he was asked what restaurant he wanted to go to for his birthday, Max said he wanted to go where he could get "fish legs!"

AZRIELA HAD TO PILE her children into the car to go get her 3-year-old from daycare. One day the 4-year-old pleaded to stay home alone. Azriela said, "Sarah, you can't stay home alone. You'd be so scared, and it's not safe." Sarah replied, "I won't be alone. God will be watching over me!"

DURING THE CAR TRIP to her sister's house, Cheryl got stopped for speeding by a state trooper. That evening while talking about the trip, Cheryl commented that they had made good time. "Yeah," Nick, 5, chimed in, "and we even stopped to visit with a policeman!"

RON AND NATHAN wouldn't help their mother around the house. She tried to shame them by saying, "I do things for you. Why, 90 percent of what I do is for others." Ron, 6, asked, "But why aren't you giving 10 percent, too?"

JALYN AND JALYSSA are twins. Jalyn was sick and missed a day of school. The next day the principal saw Jalyn, who she thought was Jalyssa. "How is your sister feeling?" the principal asked. "I am my sister!" Jalyn responded.

THE DAY AFTER TAKING her young daughters to a wedding, a mother overheard them performing a wedding ceremony for their dolls. "Do you take this man to be your awful-headed husband?" was the question asked of the pretend bride.

SETH, 2, was watching his older brothers and sister fly kites. He asked his father to help him fly a kite. Seth handed his dad the string, carried the kite outside, flattened it out and then sat on it. "OK, Daddy," Seth said, "I ready go for ride!"

CAROLYN WENT TO little Abbey's class to read a book. After the story, they started talking about flowers and how they grow and that they have to be weeded, etc. Abbey held up her hand to make a comment and Carolyn assumed she was going to say something about her family planting marigolds the weekend before. The teacher called on her and Abbey said, "Yeah, um, I'm wearing my sister's glow in the dark underwear!"

AMANDA, 7, and Evan, 4, had their friend Dillon, 6, over. Amanda said that Dillon has a bunk bed. When Monique Actman asked why Dillon has a bunk bed, he explained, "So we can have sleep-overs!" Then, Evan asked if he could sleep over, too. Dillon enthusiastically said, "Sure!" Then he added, "Mrs. Actman, you can, too, but you'll have to sleep with my dad."

CHRIS, 6, and Greg, 4, share the same bedroom. One morning at 5 a.m. their mother was awakened by voices from their bedroom. She heard Greg ask Chris where the flashlight was. Chris told him it was under the bed. Then she saw the flashlight's beam in the hallway. Getting up to investigate, she found Greg flashing the light around the bedroom. When he saw his mother Greg explained, "I just had a really good dream and I'm looking for it!"

NATHAN, 3, and his brother, Matt, were visiting their grandparents. The boys were riding their bikes on the driveway under Grandpa's watchful eye. They were getting too close to the road, and Grandpa got tired of telling the boys, over and over again, where to turn around. So he scraped a line on the gravel driveway and told them not to ride over the line. A little while later Grandpa observed that Nathan was coming to the line, getting off his bike, picking it up, carrying it over the line and continuing on his way. Grandpa realized Nathan was obeying his order. He was not riding his bike over the line — he was carrying his bike over the line!

RICKY, 3, had just ridden a two-wheel bicycle for the first time without any help from his dad. Tynan, 5, was confused by his mother's reaction. Apparently when he first learned to ride she had cried. When Ricky rode a two-wheeler for the first time she just clapped and congratulated him. Tynan went up to his mother and said, "You're supposed to cry!"

A 3-YEAR-OLD WANTING TO greet his brother came out stark naked to the school bus. When two sisters on the bus reported to their mother that evening what had happened, she asked, "Did you see anything?" The 8-year-old said, "Well, Mom, I already knew what his face looked like." The 11-year-old said, "There were so many kids at the windows, I couldn't see ANYTHING!"

WHEN NICHOLAS WAS attending kindergarten, Jayme, 2, was anxious to repeat anything he came home with. So it was no surprise when Nicholas was learning "The Pledge of Allegiance," Jayme was determined to learn it also. One day she got to the end and with a very bold voice, and her hand on her heart, she stated, "with liberty and breakfast for all!"

ROUGHHOUSING WITH YOUR SIBLING

The three "Rs" for physical fun
with your siblings are 'restling,
racing and rolling!

Dolly, 9, was roughhousing with her 1-year-old brother.

"Be careful. He's not a toy," her father said angrily.

"Yes, he is!" Dolly retorted.

"Mommy says he's a doll!"

RON, 10, and his younger brother Nathan were having an argument that was increasing in intensity. Nathan likes to get physical, while Ron is more for word strategy. As Nathan prepared to strike, Ron thought quickly and pointed to a band Nathan was wearing on his arm. The band had the letters "WWJD," which stand for "What would Jesus do?" "What about that?" Ron said, pointing to the WWJD band. Nathan looked at it for a moment, then slipped it off and prepared for battle.

A 5-YEAR-OLD CAME CRYING to his mother, saying, "He bit me on the butt!" "Well, what were you doing?" his mother asked. "I was sitting on his face!"

CATHERINE, 5, and Paul, 3, were running through the house playing super heroes. "Bang! Bang!" Paul yelled over and over again. "You can't get me. I have a bullet-proof bra!" Catherine yelled.

SPENCER, 2, was playing hide and seek, but he didn't understand the concept. When the person counting yelled, "Ready or not, here I come," Spencer yelled back, "I'm in the bedroom under the bed!"

BEN, 9, was ordering his little brother Luke around. With his hands on his hips, little Luke said angrily, "I'm not your serpent!"

KARA DECIDED TO TAKE a quick shower while Stephen, 2, was watching TV and Matthew, 7 months, was lying on a blanket on the bathroom floor. She closed her eyes while she was lathering her hair, and when she opened them, Matthew was gone! In a panic, she raced to Stephen who was intently watching TV. "Where's your brother?" she demanded. "I did hide him," Stephen cooly answered. "Show me where you put him!" Kara said, with her heart in her throat. Stephen took her to the clothes closet. The door was tightly closed. When they went inside, there was Matthew rolled up against the wall, contentedly sucking his thumb. "Stephen, did you drag him all the way in here?" Kara asked. "No, I did roll him."

CATHERINE, 9, complained that her little brother wouldn't leave her alone. She came into the room with Paul hanging on her back. "Mom, Paul's addicted to me," Catherine said.

TWO SISTERS WERE PLAYING dress-up. One announced, "I'm the damsel under stress!"

WENDY, 7, had an argument with her older brother. She got so frustrated that she stuck her tongue out at him. "Stop sticking out your tongue," her mother said. "But Mom," Wendy replied, "I didn't. I just opened my mouth and it fell out!"

KELLY, 3, tearfully complained to her father, Mike, "Robin bit me on the butt." "I did not bite Kelly on the butt," Robin said. "A mouse ran in the house and bit Kelly on the butt. Then he put a note on her butt and ran away. The note fell off and Kelly read it. It said, "I bit her on the butt just to get me in trouble!"

YET WE ARE
FAMILY FOREVER

WHEN TYNAN WAS 4, he saw two tall trees standing next to each other. "Are those trees brothers?" he asked his mother. Tynan's way of looking at the "family tree" illustrates an important point. Like trees side by side, siblings share the same soil. Their roots intertwine, and make the trees stronger as a group than they would be individually. Like trees in a forest, an orchard or a shady backyard, siblings have no choice about who will be growing beside them. But they share the same sunlight, God's love. We may have our biggest arguments with our brothers and sisters … but we also have our best laughs, our warmest hugs and our greatest support. Siblings often take different paths. Yet they cherish the same memories and, in times of need, "go out on a limb" for each other.

Siblings are a wonderful gift from God, no matter when or how they arrive. My friend Judy was telling her sons about how her youngest was born on her birthday. "Wasn't that a great birthday present!" Judy's husband said. "Yes, Jack was my birthday present," Judy said. Jack, 4, who had been sitting, quietly listening, said with a very serious look, "Did I come in a box?"

Our siblings are one of life's greatest treasures. No matter how they branch out, they are family forever.

ABOUT THE FUNNY KIDS PROJECT

The goal of The Funny Kids Project is to encourage people to savor and save the funny and heart-warming things kids say.

Children and laughter are gifts from God — enjoy!

The Funny Kids web page is at www.funnykids.com.

Come visit us to submit stories, sign up for the weekly column, order autographed books and learn about new books in the series.

ABOUT THE AUTHOR

An award-winning journalist, Grace Witwer Housholder is the wife of Terry, the mother of four and one of four siblings. She has been collecting the funny things kids say since 1987.

Her previous books are "The Funny Things Kids Say Will Brighten Any Day." Volume 1 was published in 1994, Volume 2 in 1995 and Volume 3 in 1998. Grace lives in Kendallville, Indiana, and writes for The News-Sun. Her e-mail address is tghous@noble.cioe.com.

ABOUT THE ILLUSTRATOR

An award-winning artist and pastor's wife, Debbie Rittenhouse is the wife of Jerry, the mother of four and one of five siblings. She lives in Kendallville, Indiana. Debbie's art is an example of the miracle of organ and tissue donation because corneal transplants in both eyes saved her sight. Debbie urges people to talk to their families about organ and tissue donation so that miracles such as hers can continue.

ABOUT THE DESIGNERS

Tamara Dever, owner of TLC Graphics, is the wife of Tom, mother of three (two dogs and a horse), and is the oldest of two. She's been designing books for 10 years and won her first design competition at the tender age of 10. Tamara lives in Folsom, California.

An award-winning designer, Erin Stark, owner of Stark Design Works, is the wife of Brian, mother of two, and is the oldest of two. Erin lives in Waukesha, Wisconsin.

OUR
FAMILY
STORIES

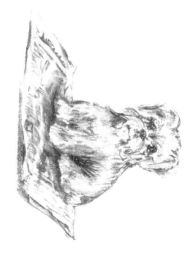

PARENT "RELEAF"

Celebrating the fun
of being a mom
or a dad

BY GRACE WITWER HOUSHOLDER

ILLUSTRATED BY DEBBIE RITTENHOUSE

"*A merry heart*
doeth good like
a medicine."

INTRODUCTION

There is no job more tiring or demanding than parenthood. Sometimes frustrations and exhaustion mount. But just when it seems unbearable — just when you are about to boil over — a child will say something so innocent, so endearing or so humorous that the only thing you can do is smile and thank God for your wonderful gift.

That's comic 'releaf' from the family tree.

Every spring trees get new leaves. The leaves enable the tree to grow and flourish. They provide refreshing shade on hot days. That's the way laughter and humor work. Laughter refreshes, reduces stress, increases creativity and builds stronger relationships. Laughter cools us down when we are about to boil over. Humor helps us grow and flourish.

New leaves are dependable. They come every spring. Humor is dependable. It's there if you look and listen.

The goal of the Funny Kids Project is to encourage people to savor and save the funny things kids say. Fill in the middle pages of this book with your own favorite stories to create a keepsake volume that you can refer to any time you need some "releaf!"

Grace Witwer Housholder
Funny Kids Project
Kendallville, Indiana, USA
www.funnykids.com

MIRROR, MIRROR ON THE WALL

Cindy's 6-year-old had just received a magic wand. He waved it over Cindy's head and said, "Abracadabra, make my mom pretty."

Cindy was taken aback. But all of a sudden he said, "Awesome, it worked!"

A MOTHER WAS BEMOANING the fact that she had found some gray hairs. "Don't worry, Mom," her little girl said. "Lots of old ladies wear their hair gray!"

STACI, 3, was watching her mother get ready for a big "night on the town." Dressed in a long, flowing green dress, Staci's mom asked Staci how she looked.

"Oh, Mommy," she said, "you look just like Kermit the Frog!"

GLENDA, 3, was watching her mother put on face cream.
"Why are you putting that on your face, Mama?" she asked.
"It's supposed to make me beautiful," her mother said.
"Well," Glenda blurted out, "they lied to you, Mama!"

AFTER HIS MOTHER had spent several hours and
lots of money at the hairdresser, Mitch asked,
"Mom, are you going to leave your hair like that?"

MOM'S WORK

On the first day of school a third-grader walked out the front door and then turned to wave goodbye to his stay-at-home mother.

"Bye, Mom," he yelled, loud enough for the whole neighborhood to hear. "Have a nice nap!"

DEBRA WAS EXPECTING COMPANY,
and she was cleaning the house from top to bottom.
Mark, 5, asked, "Who's coming to see our clean house?"

DIANE WAS TRYING TO TRIM 4-year-old Andy's bangs.
"Don't trim my eyeflashes off," he warned.

JANE WAS EMPHASIZING to her two preschoolers
that they really needed to make their beds every morning.
Mollie, 4, said, "Well, Daddy doesn't make his bed!"

A FIRST-GRADER TOLD HIS TEACHER that his mother "fixes good food, takes us places and helps us … and she's the favorite wife of my dad!"

LATE ONE NIGHT when her mother came home from work, Sarah's father told her not to bother her mother because she was pooped.
"Where?!" Sarah, 4, said looking over her shoulder.

LUCY, 6, decided to write a note to her mother who had been sick several days. But she made a grave spelling mistake. The note began: "Dead Mom … "

MOM IN THE KITCHEN

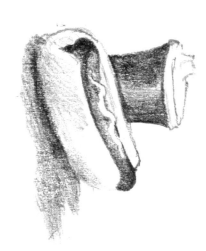

Hailey, 3, asked her mother when they would know when the cookies they had put in the oven would be done.

"Oh, I know," Hailey said, before her mother had a chance to answer. "It's when the smoke alarm goes off!"

PATRICK, 7, asked his mother if there are angels.

She said yes.

"Are they with me all the time?" he asked.

She said yes.

"Well, I tried to give one a cookie, and it fell on the floor," Patrick said.

TAMI HAD A DOZEN EGGS in the refrigerator. One of them was cracked. While Tami was on the phone Dustin, 4, got hungry and started rummaging through the refrigerator. When he found the cracked egg, he came to Tami and said very seriously, "Mom, one of your eggs is hatching!"

CATHERINE, 4, was fascinated the first time she saw fluffy white kernels bubbling out the top of the new hot air popcorn popper.

When her mother was preparing to make popcorn, she said, "Plug it in now, Mom. I want to see it throw up!"

PAUL, 3, had an incredible sweet tooth.

When his mother made brownies, she gave him two and then put the remainder in a tightly sealed container on a high shelf. A few hours later she saw Paul with a brownie smeared all over his face.

Seeing his mother's angry expression, he looked as innocent as he could and said sweetly,

"It was an accident, Mom!"

CATHERINE, 2, was happily eating crackers in the kitchen. Her mother told her to be careful and not make a mess. When her mother came back to the kitchen, she saw crumbs all over the table and floor.

"I sneezed," Catherine said.

THERE WAS ONE PIECE OF CAKE left.

"Can I cut it in half?" the mother asked.

"Sure," the 7-year-old said, "if I can have both pieces!"

PHILIPPIANS 4:13

"I can do all things through Christ which strengthens me."

MOM'S RULES

Mark, 3, finished his ice cream and demanded more.

"What's the magic word?" his mother asked.

Mark looked at his mom with a puzzled expression.

Then he said, "Abracadabra!"

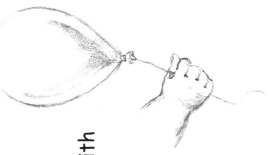

PAMELA HAD TO GIVE David, 3, a spanking … something she rarely did. As David rubbed his paddled behind he said, "You hurt my feelings!"

CHRISTINA WORKED HARD to teach good manners and polite speech to Harper, 4. One day Harper said, "Oh my God." Christina immediately told him to say, "Oh my goodness" instead. She added that saying "Oh my God" is appropriate only in prayers.
Then Harper came home with a new word — "butthead." In no uncertain terms, Christina told Harper that she didn't want to hear that word again.
"OK, Mom," Harper said, "unless I'm praying!"

A 5-YEAR-OLD who didn't like her mother's rules said, "Mom, when I'm a grownup and you're a kid — watch out!"

"MOM," a little boy said forcefully, "when our friends are here you're all nicey-nice. The minute they leave you yell your head off!"

WHEN HIS MOTHER reprimanded him for not listening, 5-year-old Corky said, "I know you are more intelligent and older and have more experience. But I know a lot of things you have forgotten!"

THINGS THAT MAKE MOM SPECIAL

Glenn, 5, was talking with a visitor

in his home. When asked,

"Where did you get those pretty

blue eyes?" Glenn thought for a moment

and replied, "God gave them to me,

and Mama put them in!"

"I LOVE YOU TO PIECES," a mother told her 2-year-old. "I love you together!" the 2-year-old said.

MICHELLE ("SHELL") WAS doing housework with 2-year-old Dylan following her. He kept trying to get his mother's attention by saying, "Mommy, Mommy, Mommy, Mommy."

Because she was so busy, Michelle said, "Stop Mommying me." Without missing a beat, Dylan said, "Shell."

SALLY STARTED TO DRIVE with a can of pop in her hand. Charlie, 6, was alarmed. "Mom," he said, "you mustn't drink and drive!"

DOLLY, 6, had an argument and put this note on her mother's pillow:

> Der Mom,
> I hat you.
> Lov, Dolly

DOROTHY LEE, 5, hurt herself. Her mother asked if she wanted some ice to ease the pain. Dorothy Lee thought a minute. "Well, yes," she said. "But could you warm it up a little?"

LUCY, 7, told her mother, "Mom, remember when you told me there is no Santa? Well, I don't believe it. I know you wouldn't go out and spend all that money on me!"

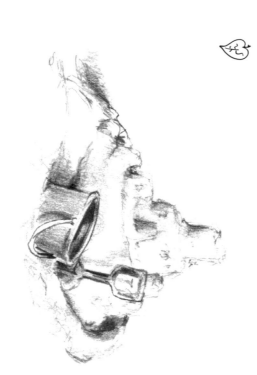

KING OF
THE CASTLE

David, 3, looked so much like his father

that everyone told him he was

"a chip off the old block."

One day he proudly told his

Grandpa Jim,

"I'm just a chip off

the old pot!"

AS THE FAMILY WAS SITTING around the supper table, Jennifer, 5, who had just started kindergarten at a Christian academy, turned to her brother, Andy, 3, and pointed to their dad.

"That's not your real father," she announced, startling the whole family.

"Yes, he is!" Andy replied.

"No, he's not," Jennifer insisted.

"God is your heavenly Father."

Then pointing at their dad, she said,

"That's your homely father!"

JACLYN, 9, was visiting her foster parents, Linda and Randy. They were in the kitchen when Randy spilled something. It was the second time he had made a mess in the kitchen that day.

"You're definitely not any good in the kitchen," Linda told Randy.

"Yes, but he's good in bed," Jaclyn said.

After a moment of stunned silence, Linda asked, "What do you mean he's good in bed?"

"Well, he goes to sleep as soon as he lies down," Jaclyn said. "You can tell because he snores so loud!"

MEGHAN, 3, had long, beautiful hair that everyone commented on because it was fixed so nicely.

One night Meghan's father, Karl, said, "I can do that," and he struggled for an hour to fix Meghan's hair.

The next morning when Paula, Meghan's mom, was fixing Meghan's hair, Meghan said,

"Daddy doesn't fix my hair very well."

"No," Paula said, "I guess not."

"That's OK," Meghan said. "He's just a dad. He'll be a mom someday!"

SCOTT, 5, asked his mom, Cathie, if there would be enough money to send him to college. Cathie said, "There is still plenty of time to plan for college, and in the meantime you could work for Daddy in the summertime."

"Oh, no," Scott said. "Daddy's going to work for me 'til the day he dies!"

•

•

ONE MORNING A THIRD-GRADER boarded the bus and gave the bus driver the largest, toothiest grin she had ever seen.

"I've got my dad's false teeth in my mouth!" the boy said. Carol, the bus driver, told him to take them back home.

"My dad never wears them. He won't miss them!" the boy said, grinning from ear to ear!

JONATHAN, 5, and Jack, 3, were supposed to be getting ready for bed, but they couldn't seem to settle down. Their father sternly sent them to their room. Their weary parents overheard Jonathan say to Jack, "Now, fold your hands this way. We HAVE to pray ... Dear Jesus, will you please give Daddy back his sense of humor in the morning!"

CALEB, 3, was overheard by his mother Kristi singing this song: "I love my daddy, I love my daddy, I love my daddy ... " When Kristi told her husband about it, he started getting warm fuzzies in his tummy thinking how sweet it was. But then Kristi said Caleb's next verse was, "BUT I DON'T KNOW WHY! NO, I DON'T KNOW WHY!" Then back to: "I love my daddy, I love my daddy ... "

BRIAN WAS ALWAYS TEASING his little sister and making her cry. His mother told him that if he did it again he would get a spanking. It wasn't long before Brian's sister was crying. Brian ran into the bedroom and crawled under the bed. At about that time Brian's dad came home and went to get Brian from under the bed. He went to the bedroom and got down on his hands and knees to find Brian.

"What's the matter, Dad?" Brian asked. "Is Mom after you, too?"

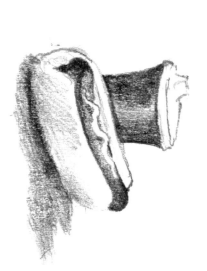

SERVING UP
SMILES

Cody, 4, was watching his father make

breakfast using hardboiled eggs.

Duane set the bowl with the peeled eggs in

front of Cody so that Cody could help cut

them up. When he cut the first egg in half,

Cody said with surprise,

"Dad, I didn't know there

was cheese inside

of eggs!"

WHEN GEORGE PLUGGED IN the family's new coffee maker, Noelle, 3, asked, "Daddy, is it raining?"

George looked out the window and said, "No."

"Daddy, are you going to make it rain?"

George said no and wondered what Noelle was talking about.

"But Daddy it's not raining."

And then George realized that she was talking about their new coffee maker which didn't "rain" like the old one.

ELIZABETH, 3 , saw her father starting to prepare breakfast. "Daddy, my doctor says I should have chocolate pudding!" she announced.

MATT WAS TELLING his daughters about exotic kinds of foods. He told them that their grandpa had eaten frog legs and octopus.

Alyssa, 5, said, "Well, I have ate elephant ears!"

WAVERLY, 4, was helping make a salad for dinner. Dart gave her a carton of sliced mushrooms and said to put half of the mushrooms in the salad because she intended to use the rest in a different dish later. When she looked at Waverly a couple of minutes later, she was surprised to see that Waverly was very carefully and deliberately breaking each mushroom slice in half, putting one half in the salad and the other half on the counter!

When all the salad ingredients were assembled, Waverly said she wanted to "mix it up."

Her father said, "That's called tossing the salad."

Dart quickly said, "No!" As literal as Waverly is, Dart did not want to see the salad tossed!

DAD AT
WORK

AT THE DINNER TABLE Don began to let off some steam that had built up from that day's office politics. His 9-year-old was surprised by his father's frustrations. "But Dad," he protested, "aren't you pretty high up in your company's anarchy?"

PATRICK, 3, put on his best pants and shirt, stuck on a tie and dragged his father's heavy briefcase to where his father was getting dressed.
"I'm ready to go to work!" Patrick said brightly.

ERIKA'S FATHER IS an aeronautical engineer. One day Erika played in the "pretend section" of her kindergarten room. That night she told her dad, "I was going to pretend that I was an engineer. Then I decided I'd rather just be a NORMAL person!"

MATT, 3, was talking to his father who was at work. While he was talking, Matt dropped the phone on the hard tile floor. Matt picked up the receiver and asked, "Dad, are you all right?"

TRACY AND ADAM, 8, were watching a show about soldiers through the centuries. Adam said he might like to be a soldier when he grows up. Tracy said her new stepdad was a soldier and Adam should talk to him before he makes up his mind. The next time Adam saw Tracy's stepdad he said, "So, Mike, Mom tells me you fought in the Civil War!"

SCOTT, 3, knew his father, a registered surveyor, had a job that included drawing pictures to earn his paycheck. When Scott was shopping with his mother, Cindy, he asked for something and Cindy said,

"No, we don't have the money today."

Scott got a puzzled look on his face. Then he asked, "Well, why doesn't Dad just draw more money?"

IT WAS A TYPICAL DAY at the Kramer house — the phone was ringing off the hook. Finally, because everyone was so busy, Steve and Jenni decided to stop answering the phone and just use the answering machine. Max, 6, overheard the conversation. A few minutes later, when the phone rang, he ran to answer it. It was one of Steve's clients. After answering the phone, Max asked, "Daddy, are you home or not?"

ALYSSA, 3, was helping her father put in a ditch beside the barn for water lines. The next day her mother mentioned that she had gotten her shoes dirty while helping her father dig the ditch.

"Daddy said it was a road," Alyssa corrected.

"It was a ditch," her mother said.

"No," Alyssa said, "Daddy kept saying, 'Get out of the road!'"

TOM TOOK CATIE, 4, to watch the airplanes at the Air Force base in Okinawa, Japan, where he was stationed. When an airplane took off, Tom told Catie, "Honey, that's the sound of freedom."

A few days later Tom and Catie were outside when a plane flew overhead. Catie looked at Tom and said, "Daddy, I like airplanes, but freedom sure is loud!"

ALLEN, 3, went to the grocery store with his dad. All through the grocery store Allen asked questions, every one starting with the query "Daddy?" Allen was very talkative at that age and could ask what seemed like a million questions in one day. When they got to the check-out, the line was very long. Allen continued with his questions, asking, "Daddy?" to start each one. This question and answer session was entertainment for the other shoppers, who were bored with waiting. Finally, Frank, tired of answering yet another question, told Allen not to call him "Daddy" again. Allen sat very quietly for a few moments. Then there was a quiet little, "Father?"

DAD AT PLAY

Little Curt enjoyed golfing with his dad.

He had a putter, but wanted a swinger.

Bill eventually had one made for him and

Curt was overjoyed.

The first time they went golfing

with Curt's new swinger he told

his dad, "I'm so excited!

I'm going to swing the

holy cow right out of myself!"

ADAM, 5, flipped on the television just as one of the NBA games between the Utah Jazz and the Chicago Bulls was ending. His father called from the other room, asking what the final score was.

"Ninety-seven to 85," Adam said.

"Who won?" his dad asked.

"Ninety-seven," Adam replied.

THE BECKER FAMILY wanted to go fishing in Michigan. The previous year Marion had found a weathered sign for the lake in the weeds and brought it home.

As the Beckers discussed how on earth they would find the lake again, Andrew said, "Gee, Dad, if you would have left the sign, we could have found the lake!"

"Children
are a gift
from God."

ELLA, 2, was watching a "Superman" cartoon with her father, Steve. "Boy, Superman sure is in some trouble!" Steve said. Turning to Ella, who was wearing Superman pajamas, Steve said, "What would you do, Superman?"

"Call Daddy!"

TERRA, 8, was excited about showing her father what her teacher had given her … a ring.

"It's a MOOD RING, Daddy!" she exclaimed.

"What does it do?" her father asked.

"It tells you the mood you're in."

"Wow, that's neat," her father said. "How does it work?"

"It just changes colors with your moods and right now … I'm unconscious!"

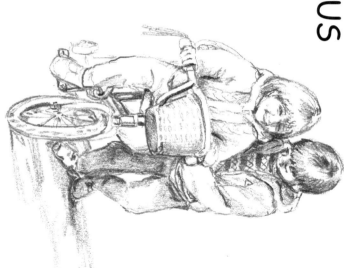

DRIVING US CRAZY

A father going through his mid-life crisis bought himself a shiny new Mustang. One day he was driving down the highway with his 5-year-old son when a police officer pulled him over. The officer calmly explained to him that he had been speeding.

The 5-year-old then loudly exclaimed, "But Officer, my daddy ALWAYS drives fast in the Mustang!"

WHEN KEVIN PICKED UP Melaney from kindergarten, she was trying to show him her artwork.

"I have to watch the road while I'm driving," Kevin said. Melaney was silent. Then she stuck the picture in Kevin's face and said, "Look at the picture, Dad. I'LL watch the road!"

GEORGE WAS DRIVING NOELLE, 3, to a friend's house. When he was halfway there, George commented that he wasn't sure of the way. David, 5, asked,

"Well, how are you going to get there?"

"I'll just follow my nose," George said.

After a moment of thought Noelle asked, "Do houses smell?"

LUKE, 6, commented, "When Daddy takes a shortcut, it always turns into a long cut."

THE FAMILY WAS DRIVING down the road when Gary became very impatient with the car ahead of him.

"Guy, I wish you'd hurry up and turn," Gary said.

"Dad, did you say guy?" 6-year-old Leslie called from the back seat.

"Yes," Gary said.

"Dad," Leslie said, "I thought you said only women drive like that!"

THE FAMILY HAD BEEN on the road all day.

Father began to yawn.

Paul, 7, called from the back seat,

"You can have my pillow, Dad!"

DAD'S COMMON CENTS

A father was explaining north, south, east and west to his 3-year-old.

"Dad, we're right in the middle, aren't we?" the boy observed.

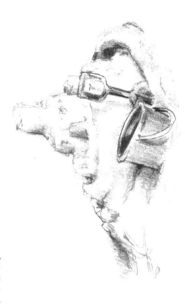

JASON NOTICED A CORVETTE that his dad had for sale in his used car lot.

"Dad," Jason said, "I'm 7 now, you know, and it's time we started looking for a car for me."

"Really?" Lance said. "What did you have in mind?"

"How much is that Corvette in your lot?"

"Twelve thousand dollars."

After a moment of silence Jason said, "If I give you the $12 now can I give you the thousand later?"

A LITTLE BOY TOLD HIS TEACHER that when he needs money he know where to find it ... under his father's chair.

DUSTIN, 8, loved all the exhibits at the Shedd Aquarium but when they got to the penguin area, he left his seat and went right up to the rail that separated the audience from the glass. It seemed like Dustin just couldn't get close enough to the penguins. Then Dustin called his father to join him. "Dad," Dustin said, pointing to the area just beyond the railing, "there's a dime down there and I can't quite reach it!"

HAIR TODAY,
GONE TOMORROW

Jeremy, 2, got a haircut. His father complimented him on how nice his new haircut looked and asked where he got his haircut.

Jeremy looked puzzled and replied, "Right here on my head!"

ZACHARY, 4, rode his bicycle with his father to get a haircut.

On the way home they rode real fast down a hill.

The wind rushed through Zach's hair.

"Dad," Zach asked anxiously, "did my new haircut blow off?"

KARL AND HIS SON, JOEY, 4, went to get haircuts.

Later Karl was joking with Joey and said, "I thought you were going to get your hair cut just like mine."

"But Mommy didn't tell them to cut it like yours," Joey said.

"Mommy, next time we go, you tell them to cut my hair just like Daddy's and make sure they cut out that spot in the back, too!"

SAMMY, 3, spent the afternoon at the zoo.
That night at the dinner table he asked his parents,
"How come in the lion family the daddy lion has so much
hair and in our family Daddy has hardly any hair?"

JACQUELINE ROSE, 3, was apprehensive when her
daddy grew a full black beard and mustache during
the holidays. She seemed a little afraid of him.
A few weeks later she was privileged to watch him shave
it all off. When it was over, Jacqueline Rose ran to her mother
and squealed with delight, "Mommy, now I got my
REAL DADDY back!"

A LOOK INTO THE FUTURE ...

Andy, 3, was bothering Jennica, 8, during a long car trip. Andy's mother asked Jennica, "Do you think Andy will EVER grow up?"

Jennica, whose father is a professional comedian, replied, "Men just grow older. They do not grow up!"

SETH, 2, thinks he and his parents are going opposite directions in the time machine. He told his mother that when she grows up she can blow bubbles in her milk with her straw. And he told his dad that when his dad becomes a little boy, Seth (who will then be grown up) will change his dad's diapers!

KYLE, 4, was told that when he grows up he'll be as tall as his father, 6 feet, 2 inches.
Kyle replied matter-of-factly, "And Daddy will be small like me!"

JAYDEN, 3, told his father, "When I get older I'm gonna be a daddy. That way when you yell at me, I can yell back!"

MITCH, 4, sternly warned his dad,
"You better watch everything you say, 'cause someday
I'm gonna talk just like you!"

MONICA, 4, was talking with her mother after watching a
local theater company's performance of Cinderella.

"Mommy," she said, "I don't want to be Cinderella when
I grow up. I just want to be a plain, ordinary princess!"

"This is the day which the Lord has made; we will rejoice and be glad in it."